CW01080617

UNWORTHY MINISTERS:
DONATISM AND DISCIPLINE TODAY

BY MARK BURKILL

The Latimer Trust

Unworthy Ministers: Donatism and Discipline Today © Mark Burkill 2010

ISBN 978-0-946307-82-1

Cover photo: Road works © Max Tactic

Published by the Latimer Trust March 2010

The Latimer Trust (formerly Latimer House, Oxford) is a conservative Evangelical research organisation within the Church of England, whose main aim is to promote the history and theology of Anglicanism as understood by those in the Reformed tradition. Interested readers are welcome to consult its website for further details of its many activities.

The Latimer Trust
PO Box 26685, London N14 4XQ UK
Registered Charity: 1084337
Company Number: 4104465
Web: www.latimertrust.org
E-mail: administrator@latimertrust.org

Contents

1. Introduction

It is not often that the 39 Articles are referred to in Anglican controversies nowadays. Not so long ago it might have been Article 17 on predestination that was cited as a reason why this doctrinal foundation of the Church of England could not be taken seriously any more. However in recent years it has been liberal Anglicans who have been in the forefront of citing Article 26 from the Anglican formularies in order to undermine the stance of orthodox, bible believing Christians.

A typical example is this from the American House of Bishops in 2004:

> The notion that the bishop's views must be in accord with those of a particular rector or congregation for the bishop to be received as chief pastor opens the way to undermining the bishop's pastoral ministry, which must embrace all and "support all baptized people in their gifts and ministries." Our theology and practice hold that ordination and consecration provide the gifts and grace necessary for the sacramental acts of a bishop to be effectual. (See article XXVI of the Articles of Religion: Of the Unworthiness of the Ministers, which hinders not the effect of the Sacraments.)[1]

When ministers and their congregations are unhappy with receiving oversight from an unbiblical and ungodly bishop this is the sort of response that is made. However we should note the way that the above statement says the bishop's

---

[1] "Caring for all The Churches" 23 March 2004 see
http://www.episcopalchurch.org/3577_32884_ENG_HTM.htm

pastoral ministry 'must embrace all.' Many congregations who cannot accept such compulsory oversight of their bishop have now sought oversight elsewhere. Does that mean they are guilty of the ancient error of Donatism, which Article 26 addresses? Other ministers and congregations may be unhappy with the leadership of their bishop, but argue that Article 26 nevertheless allows them to receive that ministry. Taken to its logical conclusion that would mean that there would be no problem with receiving confirmation or ordination at the hands of a Buddhist or Muslim bishop. These dilemmas demonstrate the need to investigate what Article 26 is and is not saying. It reveals a need to understand the real nature of Donatism. And it shows how we must think carefully about those issues in which Article 26 is referred to today.

2.   The History and Origin of Article 26

Article 26 reads as follows:

> XXVI. Of the Unworthiness of the Ministers, which hinders not the effect of the Sacrament

> Although in the visible Church the evil be ever mingled with the good, and sometimes the evil have chief authority in the Ministration of the Word and Sacraments, yet forasmuch as they do not the same in their own name, but in Christ's, and do minister by his commission and authority, we may use their Ministry, both in hearing the Word of God, and in the receiving of the Sacraments. Neither is the effect of Christ's ordinance taken away by their wickedness, nor the grace of God's gifts diminished from such as

by faith and rightly do receive the Sacraments ministered unto them; which be effectual, because of Christ's institution and promise, although they be ministered by evil men.

Nevertheless, it appertaineth to the discipline of the Church, that enquiry be made of evil Ministers, and that they be accused by those that have knowledge of their offences; and finally being found guilty, by just judgement be deposed.

The origin of this Article is readily discerned.[2] During the Reformation the concern about receiving sacraments from evil ministers is first found in the Lutheran Augsburg Confession (1530) (Article 8), where Donatism is explicitly referred to. This arrives in England through the 13 Articles of 1538 composed by Cranmer under Henry VIII (Article 5 of these). The current Article appears as Article 27 in the 42 Articles published in 1553 and is largely unchanged in Article 26 of the 39 Articles. It also appears verbatim within Article 13 of the later Irish Articles. However we must note that in the current Article (in contrast to the 13 Articles of 1538) a reference to the importance of church discipline is added in. The significance of this will become apparent below.

Griffith Thomas points out that after Augustine (354-430AD) dealt with the Donatist question the issue 'slumbered until it was revived in the Middle Ages by the gross lives of many of the Roman priests.'[3] When a renewal of Christianity and the gospel came about at the time of the

---

[2]   Gerald Bray, *Documents of the English Reformation* (Cambridge: James Clarke & Co, 1994) has the texts of the confessions quoted here. He has also written an excellent modern exposition of the 39 Articles. See Gerald Bray, *The Faith We Confess* (London: Latimer Trust, 2009).
[3]   WH Griffith Thomas, *The Principles of Theology* (Grand Rapids: Baker Book House, 1979) p367.

Reformation many sincere believers became concerned about the ministry of their church leaders. The disgust at their behaviour and the lack of effective discipline meant that many were tempted to accept the arguments of the Anabaptists who urged the importance of being baptised by a godly minister. This explains first the Lutheran and then Cranmer's concern with setting people straight over the issue of accepting sacraments at the hands of ungodly ministers. And so we can readily see why Cranmer felt it necessary to add in the paragraph about the discipline and deposition of evil ministers. He needed to reassure sincere Christians that their quite proper concerns were understood.

3.   Donatism

In order to understand the true concern of Article 26 when it speaks about the unworthiness of the minister not hindering the effect of the Sacraments it is evident that the real nature of the Donatist error must be investigated. Accusations which speak of the Donatist heresy fly around today when in truth the issue was more one of schism. Heresy is not the same as schism,[4] although certainly Augustine believed that persistent schism was a very serious matter.

The immediate origins of Donatism lie in the last great period of persecution against Christianity under the Roman Emperor Diocletian. However in 305 AD that persecution was called off and the following years saw a radical change in climate for Christianity with the acceptance

---

[4]   For an introduction to the proper significance of these terms see Gerald Bray, *Heresy, Schism and Apostasy* (London: Latimer Trust, 2008) pp45, 66.

by the Emperor Constantine of the Christian faith in 313 AD. When the Bishop of Carthage in North Africa died in 307 AD the issue of how Christians and church leaders had behaved under persecution created two different parties or tendencies within the church. There was inevitably a range of compromises that had taken place under persecution, but the handing over of copies of the Scriptures to the authorities was regarded as particularly serious. Those church leaders who had done this were known as *traditores*. When Caecilian was elected as the new bishop of Carthage some seized the opportunity to oppose him. The accusation Caecilian's opponents made was not that he himself was a *traditor* but that he had been consecrated by other bishops who were. In essence it was an accusation of 'tainted hands.'

The schism deepened when the Primate of Numidia (an area which covered part of modern Algeria) intervened. During a vacancy at Carthage he was the senior bishop in North Africa. This intervention led to a council at which Caecilian refused to appear. At that council a rival bishop called Majorinus was elected. However Majorinus soon died and in his place Donatus was elected and he held the see until 347AD.

Before long most towns in North Africa had rival bishops (Catholic and Donatist). By the time of Augustine in the late 4th and early 5th century AD the conflict was still very much alive. It is because of Augustine's efforts to tackle Donatism that we know so much about it. Augustine died in 430 AD and in the following years the people known as the Vandals occupied Carthage and North Africa. Only in the 530s did the Byzantine Empire reconquer the area. By that time the schism seems to have been healed through the weight of historical events, since the Vandals were Arians. Arianism, as a heresy, was a far more serious threat to the health of the Christian community than the schism arising from the Donatist issue. Nevertheless even in the time of Gregory the Great (590-604 AD) it was still easy to make the accusation of Donatism against dissenters from imperial and papal orthodoxy. However it is not clear whether there were real Donatists still in existence or whether this was simply a convenient accusation to make of others.

The standard reference work regarding Donatism that is cited is normally that of Frend.[5] Frend argued that the length and depth of the Donatist issue meant that it had to be explained predominantly by social factors. However since he wrote his work in 1952 that case has been substantially undermined. Alexander[6] summarises the different political and economic factors which have been said to account for the Donatist controversy. He acknowledges that Frend was correct to see the underlying issue in the controversy as being two different ways of seeing the church in relation to the world, but cautiously concludes, 'The schism cannot be explained in too narrowly religious terms. Nevertheless, it seems likely that the persistence of Donatism owes much to theology.'[7] Another recent writer states that the 'crucial advance in interpreting the history of the African schism has been the result of reasserting the overriding importance of its religious roots, and giving the nonreligious factors their due weight in this context.'[8]

---

[5]   WHC Frend, *The Donatist Church: A Movement of Protest in Roman North Africa* (Oxford: Oxford University Press, 1952).

[6]   James Alexander, "Donatism" in *The Early Christian World Volume II* (ed. Philip F. Esler; London; New York: Routledge, 2000) pp953-961.

[7]   Alexander, "Donatism," p961.

[8]   Robert A. Markus, "Donatus, Donatism" in *Augustine through the Ages: An Encyclopedia* (general ed. Allan D. Fitzgerald; Grand Rapids: Eerdmans, 1999), p285.

What then were the theological issues that emerged in addressing the Donatist issue? The presenting arguments were over matters like ordination and, most particularly, baptism. We have seen that Caecilian's election was rejected by what became the Donatist party because of his consecration at the hands of some bishops who had been *traditores*. However the primary focus of controversy was baptism. The Donatists denied the validity of baptism outside the true church and so insisted on rebaptism for those entering their community from outside.[9] Yet when Donatists entered the Catholic community they were not rebaptised.

Nonetheless, as with many theological controversies, the practical issue reflects far deeper and more significant matters. In this case it was not basic Christian beliefs as set out in the creeds, but the definition of what it means to be the church that is the central theological question. Markus demonstrates this by saying that the Donatists' 'claim to catholicity rested not on agreement with the churches in other provinces, as did the Catholics' claim, but on possession of the sacraments in their fullness and immaculate purity.'[10] Of course the issue is not quite as stark as that because both sides would have recognised the importance of doctrinal purity (through the creeds for example) as well as the importance of councils in addressing controversial questions.

It was Augustine who showed the key to dealing with the Donatist controversy. He did so from a position that had some sympathy with the North African theological tradition of purity which owed so much to Cyprian (died in 258 AD). Augustine insisted that the church was a mixed body

---

9 Markus, "Donatus, Donatism," p285.
10 Markus, "Donatus, Donatism," p286.

containing overt sinners.[11] This is why Article 26 begins with 'Although in the visible Church the evil be ever mingled with the good...' Recognising the inevitably mixed nature of Christian communities is vital and prevents anyone from pursuing unattainable goals for the church in this age. Interestingly it is possible that Augustine may actually owe this key concept in some respect to a dissident Donatist theologian called Tyconius.[12]

A problem for the position of Augustine, at least in terms of the public image of the Catholics, was that some recourse was made to the power of the state in order to tackle the Donatists. For the Donatists martyrdom was therefore a continuing experience, and this persecution was an uncomfortable reality which seemed to be the antithesis of authentic Christianity. Alexander points out how the Donatist Petilian challenged the Catholics in these terms: 'What kind of faith do you have, which does not have charity? .... Charity does not persecute.'[13] Yet the Donatists themselves seemed to lack charity when they refused to welcome back a repentant Christian or church leader, and indeed they themselves could have been accused of persecution in the way they dealt with Caecilian originally.

At this distance in time it is difficult to assess the truth, but it may be that as the 4th century church worked out its new relationship to the imperial power there was indeed a laxity in tackling ungodly leadership in the church. As we have seen already, this often appears to be the problem that leads people to take up a Donatist or Anabaptist type position.

---

[11] Markus, "Donatus, Donatism," p286.
[12] Markus, "Donatus, Donatism," p286; Alexander, "Donatism," p967.
[13] Alexander, "Donatism," p966.

The principle of the church being mixed and that even 'sometimes the evil have chief authority in the ministration of the Word and Sacraments' is a reality that Christians must accept if their witness to the gospel is to be maintained in a healthy way. However that is no excuse for not addressing the issue of discipline. Those who fling around accusations of Donatism would be wise to recognise what Augustine himself said, according to the Augsburg confession, 'Neither must we subscribe to catholic bishops if they chance to err, or determine anything contrary to the canonical divine Scriptures.'[14]

This reminds us that Donatism is not about doctrine and false teaching, but about behaviour that is unworthy of Christ and the gospel, and dealing with its consequences in the Christian fellowship. Augustine condemned Pelagians and Arians and considered it essential to divide from such heretics. And of course the Donatists would have agreed and responded in the same way to such groups. Donatism was fundamentally a misguided attempt to preserve the purity and holiness of the Christian community. To repudiate the past fellowship and ministry of those who had sincerely repented of their sin in betraying Christ under persecution denies the love and charity that followers of Christ are called to. However it was not, and is not, wrong to be concerned about the purity and holiness of the church, as indeed Augustine himself was.

Article 26 is certainly about Donatism, but because the real nature of Donatism is misunderstood today we must

---

[14] Augsburg confession in, for example, Bray, *Documents*, p648. Intriguingly the Augsburg confession actually wrongly attributes the quotation to Augustine's treatise against Petilian's epistle, whereas in fact it is from *Ad Catholicos* 'To Catholic Brothers' Chapter 28. I am most grateful to Peter Sanlon for working this out.

now turn to the part of the Article which is not about Donatism. The last paragraph of Article 26 is about discipline and this is the key issue that is so often ignored and neglected today.

4.   Discipline

To call for discipline in the church in the way that Article 26 does in its last paragraph does not mean one is a Donatist. Indeed one ought to argue that by insisting on the necessity of discipline and the deposition of 'evil ministers' the church will be preserved from the heartache of schism arising from the toleration of heresy and immorality. The exposition of the 39 Articles by Boultbee explains why the discipline of ungodly ministers must not be neglected.[15] In regard to the first part of Article 26 he says that the Article 'might offer an answer theoretically and theologically true; but it could not control those instincts and sympathies which really govern the majority of mankind in such matters.'[16] Boultbee was referring to the way in which certain pious clergy were silenced for nonconformity in the controversy over royal supremacy and their congregations were then commanded to attend the Parish Church which they found served by clergy whose morality and biblical understanding were poor. He therefore says that practically speaking 'no Church can long maintain the loyalty and affection of its members, excepting

---

[15]   T.P. Boultbee, *A Commentary on the Thirty-Nine Articles* (London: Longmans, Green and Co, 1893).
[16]   Boultbee, *Commentary*, p222.

by the personal character and influence of an enlightened and pious clergy.'[17]

Thus Boultbee concludes, in a statement that is frequently quoted by subsequent evangelical expositions of this Article, that while Article 26 maintains a doctrine of great importance (i.e. addressing the Donatist error) 'it is contrary to reason, to experience, to history, to Scripture, to suppose that an ungodly, still less a vicious, ministry can issue in anything but an ungodly and corrupt state of the people. No conspicuous work of grace has shown itself apart from a faithful, devoted, prayerful administration of the word and ordinances of Christ.'[18]

Prior to the Reformation Wycliffe and his followers were distressed by ungodly clergy. There are those who accuse Wycliffe of Donatism.[19] However one wonders whether Wycliffe's concerns and writings are in fact being misunderstood for the reasons that Boultbee expresses so well (the frustration of sincere Christians with a lack of disciplinary measures being taken against ungodly clergy). There are signs that modern writers are not so sure that he can be accused of Donatism. Thus Levy concludes an overview of Wycliffe's eucharistic theology by saying, 'Perhaps scholars will have to be content to say that there were times when Wyclif had been orthodox, times when a Donatist, and other times still when he had walked a perilous path between.'[20] Yet the modesty of even this diluted accusation that Wycliffe was a Donatist ought to be

---

[17] Boultbee, *Commentary*, p222.
[18] Boultbee, *Commentary*, pp222-3.
[19] A.P. Forbes, *An Explanation of the Thirty-Nine Articles* (London: Parker and Co, 1890), p480 and *The Tutorial Prayer Book* (ed. Charles Neil & J.M. Willoughby; London: The Harrison Trust, 1913), p563 are examples.
[20] Ian Levy, "Was John Wyclif's Theology of the Eucharist Donatistic?," *Scottish Journal of Theology* 53 (2000): p153.

questioned. Levy himself reminds us that Wycliffe was known as 'Doctor Augustinus' and how his writings show extensive awareness of the danger of Donatism. In fact it may be possible to clear Wycliffe entirely of the accusation of Donatism if one is able to read his writings without doing so through the prism of the transubstantiation issue. When Wycliffe got to the point of declaring that a priest in mortal sin does not consecrate the host[21] he is not necessarily being a Donatist, since his view of what any priest does with the bread and wine has changed and he is stressing the worthy reception of the elements instead.

In addressing the issue of discipline one must consider how that discipline is to be exercised. Article 26 plainly envisages the leadership of the Church taking on this difficult and painful responsibility. Some may be reluctant to do this because they desire the Christian community to be as open and inclusive as possible to outsiders. However the very existence of the term 'heresy' implies the existence of boundaries and if unfaithful ministry is not dealt with then the foundations of the Church's existence are undermined. All parties in the sixteenth century would of course have been agreed on that and would have been amazed if they were accused of Donatism in desiring to exercise discipline.

Today the reality in the Church of England and elsewhere in the Anglican Communion is that the leadership of the Church in some provinces will not take on the responsibility of discipline. Various cases such as the 1996 Righter trial have demonstrated there is no will to deal with heretical teaching.[22] There is thus little recourse for clergy and congregations who are not Donatists and yet are fearful

---

[21]   Levy, "John Wyclif's Theology," p151.
[22]   See for example http://anglicansonline.org/archive/news/articles/1997/righter.html

of the consequences of a lack of discipline with regard to heresy among ministers. Bray says this about the current situation: 'It can be safely concluded that no appeal to the formularies or judicial organs of the Church of England in a matter of heresy is likely to succeed, and that anyone who tried such a thing would be blackballed and effectively driven out of the church, either by those of a different persuasion or by those who do not want to rock the boat.'[23]

If this is the case, then the only option available to clergy and congregations when faced with evil ministry at a parish or diocesan level is to refuse fellowship with such ministers. Manifestations of such fellowship or its breach are various, but the most painful area will be the reception of Holy Communion. It is notable that the storm centre for the issue of Donatism is baptism, the sacrament of initiation into the fellowship of Christians. However the storm centre for the issue of discipline is the sacrament of the Lord's Supper, the sacrament of fellowship among Christians. When Richard Baxter addresses the issue of ungodly and unworthy ministers in his Christian Directory it is not so much the issue of baptism that calls forth many words from his fertile mind, but that of communion.[24]

In practical terms the refusal to share the bread and wine of Christ's death with fellow Anglican ministers who teach or practise ungodliness may be painful and disruptive. Yet when it is a bishop who is exercising the ungodly ministry which makes such fellowship impossible, even graver problems emerge because of the role the bishop has

---

[23]   Bray, *Heresy*, p61.
[24]   Richard Baxter, *The Practical Works of Richard Baxter Volume 1: A Christian Directory in Four Parts* (London: George Virtue, 1846), p498. Here we find Baxter tackling in relation to the Lord's Supper the question 'May we lawfully receive this sacrament from an ungodly and unworthy minister?'

for confirmations, ordinations and institutions of new ministers. This is when the tear in the fabric of communion which arises over the lack of godly discipline becomes most evident. It has been seen in recent years at the highest level of the Anglican Communion when the Primates have met from Dromantine 2005 onwards[25].

Whenever the question of discipline is raised then we tend to find that behind it lies the issue of comprehensiveness. Often the reluctance to exercise appropriate discipline along the lines of Article 26 stems from a misapprehension and an unhistorical reading of the Anglican commitment to comprehensiveness. Jim Packer has shown how comprehensiveness has been extolled as an Anglican virtue from at least four distinct points of view since the mid nineteenth century[26]. Such confusion could explain why not only church leaders decline to exercise such discipline but also why the last resort form of discipline as exercised by the refusal of fellowship and communion is regarded with such distaste.

The Anglican commitment to comprehensiveness does not mean that sin does not matter. Error and immorality are important and must be tackled. That is why the ordinal speaks of the responsibility of church leaders (both bishops and other clergy) 'to banish and drive away all erroneous and strange doctrine contrary to God's Word.' That is why the Prayer Book envisages care being taken about admission to communion. However comprehensiveness does mean that the Church of England will not view the visible Church as

---

[25] For the Communiqué from Dromantine see
http://www.anglicancommunion.org/acns/news.cfm/2005/2/24/ACNS3948.
And note the Church Times report of 4 March 2005.
[26] Jim Packer, *Anglican Evangelical Identity: Yesterday and Today* (London: Latimer Trust 2008), pp143-161.

being coterminous with its own denomination. This principle of comprehensiveness will also readily acknowledge that those disciplined for heresy or immorality are still within the bounds of the visible Church.[27] And of course comprehensiveness is further reflected in the acknowledgement that the evil of certain ministers does not invalidate all that they do. In this way the error of Donatism is avoided.

Nonetheless the Anglican understanding of comprehensiveness still includes a commitment to discipline along the lines of the second part of Article 26. And the standard by which that discipline is exercised is of course God's Word. Appropriate discipline according to God's Word is what maintains the health and unity of the Church, as well as marking the appropriate boundary between the Church and the world. In 1 Corinthian 5:9-11 the apostle Paul makes it clear that association and eating with immoral unbelievers is not wrong, but that it is wrong for those who profess to be followers of Christ.

If discipline is not exercised according to God's Word then other means have to be found to keep the visible Church together. In recent years it has become all too obvious that the instrument for doing this has to be canon law. In modern disputes within the Anglican Communion it is remarkable how the more liberal leadership has insisted on the strictest adherence to canons while ignoring the teaching of Scripture. This precisely inverts the biblical position in which rules for ordering the church are seen as the servants of biblical truth. A recent example of this within the Church of England is cited by Gerald Bray: 'The bishop of Southwark saw fit to

---

[27] D Holloway, *The Reform of the Episcopate and Alternative Episcopal Oversight* (Reform, 1996 & 1998) – available on the Reform website www.reform.org.uk

revoke the licence of one of his clergy who had called a South African bishop to ordain men for a church plant (which Southwark had repeatedly refused to do) but has done nothing to discipline the liberal clergy in his diocese, not least the dean of his cathedral, who has publicly compared orthodox Christians to the Taliban.'[28]

Tyranny and persecution is the inevitable result of trying to make commitment to canons rather than Scripture the basis of church discipline. That is why another Article (6) warns that 'Holy Scripture containeth all things necessary to salvation: so that whatsoever is not read therein, nor may be proved thereby, is not to be required of any man, that it should be believed as an article of the Faith, or be thought requisite or necessary to salvation.' And furthermore Article 20, while acknowledging the need for the visible Church to order itself, declares 'it is not lawful for the Church to ordain any thing that is contrary to God's Word written.'

While Judith Maltby makes some pertinent and useful observations about the operation of the 1993 Act of Synod which created 'flying bishops' (passed after the votes in General Synod in 1992 in favour of the ordination of women), she ends up with the remarkable statement that opposing this Act represents the true understanding of Anglican comprehensiveness[29]. It is telling that in quoting Article 26 she ignores the second part referring to discipline. Her main argument for the repeal of the Act of Synod is that it is dangerous to elevate conscience over a catholic understanding of orders.[30] However this ignores the fact that

---

[28] Bray, *Heresy*, p85.
[29] Judith Maltby, "One Lord, One Faith, One Baptism, but Two Integrities?" p58 in *Act of Synod – Act of Folly?* (ed. Monica Furlong; London: SCM, 1998) pp42-58.
[30] Maltby, "One Lord," p47.

it is dangerous to elevate either conscience or orders over Scripture. This is why Article 20 warns about the Church ordaining something contrary to God's Word written. If a conscience that is seeking to submit to the authority of Scripture is not accommodated by the order of the Church then the consequences are very grave. An erroneous understanding of comprehensiveness leads ironically to a liberal form of Donatism which expels godly Christians from the fellowship of the Church. If Scriptural discipline is not exercised by church leaders and the commitment to comprehensiveness is read unhistorically then how are those who dissent on the ground of Scripture to be treated? Are they to be treated as Christians? Are they to be persecuted? Persecution of such Christians is in fact the symptom of an illiberal Donatist spirit.

5.   Modern Issues

We are now in a position to consider various modern controversies in which the teaching of Article 26 is pertinent or has been quoted.

5.1   Rebaptism

In evangelical Christianity the proper administration of baptism is widely misunderstood. While strict baptists have historically sought to justify rebaptism on grounds which relate to their gathered church theological principles, rebaptism has now become widespread in many other circles. It is often practised when someone makes an adult profession of Christian faith after being baptised as a child, but it may be administered even when someone has already been baptised as a teenager in a baptist church. Those who offer rebaptism in such circumstances are probably unconscious of any commitment to a Donatist position but such practice is certainly indicating the belief that there is something defective in the earlier administration of baptism. If it was not the minister or church that was at fault then the only other possibility is ultimately God himself. That is why Anglican clergy should not be involved in rebaptism. While this modern plague of rebaptism really stems from a failure to understand how baptism is signifying the gospel of forgiveness of sins through Christ, it does show the poverty of much evangelical thinking about the visible Church and an ignorance of the lessons of the Donatist controversy.

5.2   GAFCON and the Fellowship of Confessing Anglicans

Following the Global Anglican Future conference (GAFCON) in Jerusalem in June 2008 a Declaration was issued[31]. Within this, point 13 has been subject to particular criticism. This states 'We reject the authority of those churches and leaders who have denied the orthodox faith in word or deed. We pray for them and call on them to repent and return to the Lord.' It has been said that this presupposes the existence of a real split or schism. That is certainly true. However it seems that many will not take practical disciplinary steps in response to the crisis over the gay issue within the Anglican Communion until certain leaders declare through a formal procedure that this split does exist.

---

[31]   See the Jerusalem Declaration in *Being Faithful* (London: Latimer Trust, 2009) pp6-7.

Of course there may be questions over who has the authority to say that there is a real problem. Yet if leaders fail to act to discipline immorality and unbiblical teaching then godly Christians, whom they are supposed to be leading, will act by other means. When at least 300 bishops of the Anglican Communion are convinced there is a real problem then the issue cannot be dismissed by taking refuge in accusations of Donatism.

A typical example of confused thinking on this issue came out of a discussion on the Fulcrum website shortly after GAFCON. Article 26 was quoted and then the contributor said,

> I can't help wonder whether it is Gafcon's desired intention to invoke the last bit about deposing ministers, whilst forgetting the initial point that the nature of the minister has (hath) no effect on the efficacy of the sacrament. This is why I find myself in a cleft stick, as I would happily receive the grace of the sacrament from (say) Gene Robinson, since he has been ordained and consecrated as a minister of the sacraments in God's church (paragraph 1), but I am probably in agreement with many individuals at Gafcon when it comes to the personal sexual morality of such ministers.[32]

The contributor is to be congratulated on quoting the Article in full, with both of its paragraphs. However one does not need to ignore what the first part is saying while nonetheless insisting on the need for discipline. It is a scandal and blight on the witness of the church if anyone is placed in the position of having to receive baptism, let alone communion, from an unorthodox and ungodly pastor, and in particular

---

[32] Tim Goodbody, Fulcrum, 1 July 2008. See www.fulcrum-anglican.org.uk

from a bishop. It is not a situation that should be tolerated and point 13 from the Jerusalem Declaration is simply recognising that this is a scandal.

5.3   Women Bishops

In many provinces of the Anglican communion women bishops have been introduced with no effective provision of adequate oversight for those who believe that this is both unScriptural and contrary to catholic tradition. However in the Church of England there are currently attempts to make some provision for such dissidents, following on the existing provision made in an Act of Synod after the vote to allow the ordination of women as presbyters in 1992. Nevertheless those charged with establishing the framework of provision for those who cannot accept women bishops are finding that this is a very difficult task. The reason for this is precisely those issues surrounding the Donatist controversy and it is not surprising to find Article 26 being quoted in this context.

The critique by Judith Maltby of the operation of the Act of Synod has already been referred to.[33] I do not believe her understanding of Anglican comprehensiveness is correct, however I do believe there is considerable justification in many of her comments. She sees the ultimate basis of extended episcopal oversight offered in the Act of Synod as being the need to avoid physical contact with bishops or male priests who have participated in the laying on of hands. In her opinion it is hard to avoid calling this 'modern Donatism' or a 'theology of taint.'[34]

---

[33]   p16 above.
[34]   Maltby, "One Lord," p55.

However because she operates with a predominantly 'catholic' understanding of the church she does not appreciate the basis of the evangelical case for adequate provision. She certainly notes the incongruity in making provision for the conscience of those opposed to the ordination of women and not doing so for those opposed to bishops who take a liberal stance on human sexuality.[35] She also states that the Church of England has never responded to differing doctrinal views by setting up an extended or alternative sacramental system. She says, 'Your bishop can deny the resurrection, the Trinity, and the incarnation; he may be a racist, liar or thief – but no one will offer you a PEV' (Provincial Episcopal Visitor or 'flying bishop').[36]

This is all true, but she never addresses the obvious evangelical response to this situation and indeed the consequences of that for the issue of women priests and women bishops. Thus the evangelical will note that the lack of doctrinal discipline is exactly the issue and is precisely what causes the problems which face those charged with framing legislation in this matter. It is not a case of provision for Christian conscience on the one hand versus maintenance of catholic order on the other. The real issue is whether the church will teach and live under the authority of God's word or not. This applies not only to the woman bishop who in her person embodies unfaithfulness to Scripture, but far more importantly to the issue of the acceptability of homosexual behaviour (or theft for that matter) and to denials of the resurrection and incarnation.

It is notable that when Judith Maltby quotes from Article 26 she omits any mention of the last paragraph

---

[35] Maltby, "One Lord," pp56-58.
[36] Maltby, "One Lord," p56.

concerning the importance of discipline and this is never addressed in her article. In a similar vein correspondence in the Church Times in January 2009 contained this comment on the way provision for dissidents was being made: 'This is modern Donatism. The Donatists repudiated the episcopal ministration of those whom they regarded as having betrayed the Catholic Church. They were answered by Augustine of Hippo with the theology that underlies Article XXVI. Such heresy should have no part in the Catholic ordering of our Church.'[37] Again there is no reference to the application of church discipline and the authority of Scripture, and in fact the dissidents are effectively labelled heretics. We have already seen that this is a questionable description of the Donatist controversy and therefore it is probably those who wish to drive out of the church any who maintain a position that is established by Scripture and in line with tradition that deserve the label Donatist.

All who seek support from Article 26 and the Donatist controversy in order to minimise provision for opponents of these innovations in women's ministry would do well to remember that Augustine was careful not to lose sight of wider issues in this. While writing in connection with Donatist matters he also says, 'Neither must we subscribe to catholic bishops if they chance to err, or determine anything contrary to the canonical divine Scriptures.'[38] In other translations 'subscribe' is translated 'obey.'[39]

Gerald Bray points out that the provision for those who cannot accept women bishops will indeed introduce a form of schism but he stresses that 'the resulting division will come about because the majority in the church is not

---

[37] Jean Mayland, Church Times, 16 Jan 2009.
[38] See Augsburg confession in Bray, *Documents*, p648.
[39] See http://augsburgreader.blogspot.com/2006/11/article-xxviii.html

prepared to maintain its traditional teaching and practice.... If a 'schism' of this kind develops in England, it will not be because a minority has broken away from the church but because the current majority in it has not remained faithful to the teaching of Scripture.'[40] Once again we recall how Article 20 warns us about the dangers of the Church ordaining something which is contrary to God's Word.

5.4   Consequences of an unbiblical 'wedding'

The failure of bishops and church authorities to discipline what Article 26 calls 'Evil Ministers' is seen in many parts of the Anglican Communion today. In the absence of such discipline clergy and congregations have no other course of action save that of declaring that a breach in fellowship now exists. A typical example took place in the diocese of London in 2008.

On 31st May the Revd Martin Dudley conducted a service of blessing at St Bartholomew the Great in the City of London for two male Anglican clergy following their civil partnership ceremony. This was referred to as a 'wedding' in some press reports.[41] Although the Bishop of London investigated the case, no disciplinary action was taken against Martin Dudley. Thus when the City of London Deanery Synod next met in October 2008 the synod representatives of three evangelical churches (including the lay chair of the synod) felt obliged to make a statement[42] in which they made it clear that their fellowship with Revd Dudley was fractured because of this action.

---

[40]   Bray, *Heresy*, p72.
[41]   See the form of service available at http://www.reformlondon.org.uk
[42]   See for example http://www.anglican-mainstream.net/?p=5219   Statement made at City of London Deanery Synod.

Martin Dudley's response to this raised the issue of Donatism and in particular said this to those who had made that statement:

> We become Donatists if we doubt the faithfulness and promises of God. We do it if we think the Gospel is ours and not the Gospel of Jesus Christ. We do it if we think we, and we alone, are the good seed and everyone who does not agree with us is no better than weeds. If we take that approach, then we must scrutinize the life and behaviour and connections of everyone. At the door of the church-building those who should be welcoming will be required to ask questions about what each person has thought and said and done in the past week.[43]

Much of what Martin Dudley says about Donatism and its rigorism is true yet he fails to point out that there was no disagreement between Catholics and Donatists over the fact that sinful behaviour had to be recognised as such and dealt with. The disagreement, as we have seen, was really over how such behaviour was to be dealt with, and in particular after that behaviour had been repented of. Augustine and the historic Anglican tradition are certainly committed to a comprehensive church where 'the evil be ever mingled with the good' but this is not the comprehensiveness that Martin Dudley imagines.

Sinful behaviour has to be disciplined where it is public and unrepentant because sin matters to God so much that his Son died on the cross to redeem us from it. Martin Dudley needs to state honestly whether he regards homosexual behaviour as sinful in the eyes of God and

---

[43] Response by Martin Dudley 19 October 2008 can be viewed at http://www.peter-ould.net/2008/10/19/martin-dudley-mishandles-donatism

whether he wishes to bless that in God's name. Those who have the painful responsibility of disciplining Anglican clergy must also ask themselves whether homosexual behaviour is sinful in the eyes of God. If it is, then doing nothing about those who teach and act to the contrary is a dereliction of duty. Those who have no authority or power to discipline clergy in this matter can only respond as those evangelical churches did in this case, and others should not be surprised by this. The failure to discipline immorality in the Christian church creates schism. That has been the consequence of this unbiblical 'wedding' and similar actions in other parts of the Anglican Communion. To seek discipline for immorality is not to be Donatist, as Article 26 demonstrates.

5.5   Ordinations and Institutions

In the Anglican tradition ordinations of new ministers and the institution or licensing to new churches are done by bishops. In recent years orthodox Christian ministers in the Church of England have faced a growing dilemma when they seek ordination or institution at the hands of a bishop who is known to affirm unbiblical teaching or behaviour. It is the dilemma which Article 26 addresses.

On the one hand orthodox ministers are generally happy to be ordained by such a bishop for the reason that their ordination is certainly not invalidated by the false teaching of such a bishop. However the problem is that such ordinations (and institutions) are generally conducted in such a fashion that these services appear to be an expression of unbroken fellowship between the bishop and the minister.

Ordinations and institutions can be performed privately and have been so done on numerous occasions in the past. In such instances the public expression of fellowship is minimal. However there seems to be little desire by the bishops in these cases to accommodate the consciences of those who do believe their fellowship with them has been broken. This was seen in a case in the diocese of Chelmsford in 2007. An ordinand was willing to be publicly ordained by the Bishop of Chelmsford despite that bishop's well known support for unbiblical teaching on the matter of human sexuality.[44] However this ordinand did not want to share in Holy Communion with the diocesan bishop following his ordination, since that was an expression of Christian fellowship with him. On learning this the bishop refused to ordain the individual concerned. He quoted the rubric in the 1662 ordinal which says, 'Then shall the Bishop proceed in the Communion, and all that are ordered shall tarry, and receive the Holy Communion the same day with the Bishop.'

There is no way of knowing whether this has always been practised, though of course it should be under normal circumstances. What is notable in this case, as in other recent controversies, is how a bishop is willing to quote rubrics and canons and insist on obedience to them, while not himself obeying God's Word.

---

[44] Reference is made to J Gladwin's position as Patron of Changing Attitude in this report http://www.guardian.co.uk/uk/2007/jul/18/religion.gayrights and in Mike Reith's statement at http://chelmsfordanglicanmainstream.blogspot.com /2007/07/vicar-of-dagenham-issues-statement-on.html

6.   Conclusion

Article 26 may be misused or misunderstood but it is actually a word of much wisdom in circumstances where unorthodox and unworthy leadership among God's people has created division and confusion. It is therefore very much a word for today within the Anglican Communion.

Those who accuse others of Donatism nowadays often have no idea of what this error really involved. And those who make such wild accusations while ignoring the need to discipline heretical teaching must remember that Article 26 has that paragraph on discipline for a good reason. It is there because schism is bound to arise where there is no will to 'banish and drive away erroneous and strange doctrines.' In fact a denomination which does not take discipline seriously is liable to persecute and unchurch those who know that heretical teaching must be tackled for the sake of the health of God's people. Such illiberal liberalism can be fairly accused of a Donatist rigour itself.

Some imagine that Article 26 means that the ministry of unorthodox bishops and clergy can be accepted without qualms. They too need to note that the first paragraph of the Article should not be separated from the second. It is not that ordinations by an ungodly bishop, or baptisms by an ungodly minister are invalid, it is rather that outward manifestations of Christian fellowship when there is in reality no such gospel fellowship present are deeply confusing for God's people. Glossing over the problem does not honour Christ and indeed is not good for the spiritual welfare of such church leaders. It is possible for a bishop who is a false teacher to ordain and institute clergy in private, and that might satisfy the conscience of those who know they are not in communion with such a church leader. However when that bishop ministers in public, those who are not in communion with him surely need to find some means of demonstrating the reality of that broken fellowship. Biblical Christians may find themselves disagreeing about the precise manner in which that broken fellowship is practically manifested, but they will agree about the principle of exercising discipline in this way.

Yet there are also those who do need to be warned about the dangers of Donatism. A proper concern for the purity of the church may lead Christians into absurd and uncharitable positions. There are plenty of examples of this in church history other than the Donatists themselves. Augustine's insistence that the church is a mixed body in which 'the evil be ever mingled with the good' must be taken seriously. Purity is a proper concern for Christians but if it leads someone to break fellowship with orthodox Christians, then it has become arrogance and pride.

LATIMER PUBLICATIONS

LATIMER PUBLICATIONS

LATIMER PUBLICATIONS